MOSAICS

Made From Beautifully Broken Pieces

by

**Visionary
Deborah A. Franklin**

Coauthors

Pixie Lee
Chiara Noble
MaDonna Williams
Delphia Sheila Marshall
Jackie 'Lady J' Miller
J C Gardner

© 2021 by Deborah Franklin Publishing. All rights reserved.

No part of this book may be reproduced in any written, electronic, recording, or photocopying without written permission of the publisher or author. The exception would be in the case of brief quotations embodied in the critical articles or reviews and pages where permission is specifically granted by the publisher or author.

Although every precaution has been taken to verify the accuracy of the information contained herein, the author and publisher assume no responsibility for any errors or omissions. No liability is assumed for damages that may result from the use of information contained within.

Contents

Introduction — 1
Pixie Lee

No Longer The Shadow — 14
Deborah A. Franklin

Take It All, But Not My Baby! — 20
Chiara Noble

Healing From The Inside Out — 34
MaDonna Williams

It's More Than Just A Journey — 45
Delphia Sheila Marshall

Kept By His Grace — 60
Jackie 'Lady J' Miller

Reclaiming Your Destiny — 76
J C Gardner

Introduction

Pixie Lee

It would be easy to say that we've all had our challenges. We've all had life to happen to us. But the question is how have we all dealt with life happening to us? Well, let's take a journey. I can tell you it has taken a lot for me to get to this point that I'm at in my life. I never thought that I would be a 3x published author, certified life coach, mentor, ghost writer, publisher and part owner in a TV network and a co-host of a TV show. Some of these things never even crossed my mind ever. But that's the funny thing about life; no matter what you've planned, God will take you completely off course to get you to where He wants and needs you to be.

Let me tell you about my journey to how I got here. For those that don't know, I'm a PK (preacher's kid), a badge I wear now with honor. But there used to be a day where I didn't want anyone to know. It was never cool being the PK. We were the butt of jokes and anything we did or said that people thought wasn't PK Approved, we then were judged for what we were doing. It was a real hard tag to wear at the age of 16. As I began to navigate life, certain challenges were thrown at me. The first big challenge was being diagnosed with migraines at the age of 16. They were so debilitating and painful, I couldn't do anything but lay in the bed in the dark and cry until I could throw up and it would finally go away. I would never know when they were coming on, they would just show up. Looking back at it now, I wouldn't feel like myself when I would wake up which should have been a clue that something was wrong but who thinks like that at 16? By age 17, I was dealing with asthma. Sounds like fun, huh? Well, it was about as much fun as watching a football game in the rain. Little did I know this journey would continue the rest of my life.

As I entered young adulthood, I was still battling my migraines and I felt like they would never end. I literally felt like life as I knew it would never return to pre-migraine life. You see, my migraines made it difficult to enjoy life and family because I never knew when they would show up. At this stage in my life, I wasn't able to function for days at a time. The doctor I was seeing thought the solution was to keep me medicated. By the time I was pushing back on my treatment, I was a wife, a mother, had a full-time job and was going to school so being heavily medicated for days at a time was not an option for me. My husband at the time understood but my 2-year-old son, 4-year-old daughter and 6-year-old daughter did not. All they knew was mommy was in a lot of pain and didn't know why.

In my natural rebellious way, I figured I would just stop taking the medication. Well, that didn't work, and it didn't last long. My migraines had started progressing and new side effects and symptoms were emerging. I remember driving without sunglasses as I often did, and the sun hit my eyes the wrong way and triggered a migraine as I was driving and talking to my mom on the phone. I began to cry, and she began to panic and pray all at the same time. I can't remember how I got home, I just know God sent his angels of protection around me and I made it safely home and my children weren't in the car with me, so they didn't have to see mommy in pain and turmoil. See after my migraine started, my tongue began to swell. I started seeing black spots in my vision and it was blurry. The pain was unbearable. Being able to get home was definitely God. So finally, someone suggested that I change doctors. Now I can't understand for the life of me why that never crossed my mind, but I was too busy being mad and upset over my situation. When I found out my dad also suffered from migraines but outgrew them, I was even upset at him for a second. But then reality set in and I was just mad I had them and jealous that I was unable to get rid of them.

Now a new journey began as I found a new doctor at Emory Neurology. I must admit I was skeptical when I started working with this doctor because I felt like everyone would tell me the same thing. That was absolutely not the case. I was paired with an absolute angel. I'm sure she didn't want to take my case on. I know I wasn't the most pleasant patient she's ever had, but I was tired of everything and I was convinced everything she suggested wouldn't work.

Her approach was much different from my last doctors. She started with research. She asked me about my migraines and symptoms and then she began to ask me questions about my body and day-to-day activities leading up to my migraines. She asked questions like, "What did you eat the day before?" or "How much rest did you get?" And "Do you have any stressful situations going on at the moment?" When I say shocked does not even begin to cover how I was feeling or the look that was probably on my face. It was at that moment I knew we would find new answers and a new treatment path. But that doesn't mean it was easy. I had to keep a journal and figure out my triggers. My journal went on for maybe 6 months or a little shorter. But when I returned, I had answers to her questions. I now knew what foods would trigger my migraines. I knew what lack of sleep and stress would do to my body. I also knew my monthly played a part in my migraines too. So, let me give you some free advice. If you suffer from migraines that literally take over your life, please get a doctor who is willing to get in the trenches with you and figure them out with you. Everyone's body is different, and it just may take some time to unpack that suitcase.

We were able to come up with a treatment plan and it worked. I was more receptive to take medication this time because I also was armed with a game plan. And the medication that I was on this time wasn't the medication that I was previously using so it wasn't keeping me groggy and in the bed for days at a time. I'm happy to say I was headache free for 2 years before I was hit with the worse headache of my life. I know at this point you're wondering why is she telling us all this background? It's simple: you have to understand the story before you can understand my shout.

So many times, while we are in the struggle, we're just asking and sometimes begging God to get out of it, that we miss the lessons and blessings as we are going through it. I was on roller-coaster ride after the 2 years of being headache free and it showed up in my headaches. My home life was different, my work life was different. My children were older--just a laundry list of things going on. On June 28, 2016, I woke up with the worst migraine I had ever had in my entire life. I knew this one was nothing like any migraine I had ever had before. I knew in the back of my mind that the things I would normally do to get rid of them wasn't going to work this time. It just felt different. And I was right. I had this headache for about 5 days before I finally went to the emergency room. They gave me the standard migraine cocktail: Benadryl, morphine and something else. I can't remember exactly what that third drug was, but when all of them are given to you through an IV, let me tell you, the sleep and relief you experience is unexplainable. While this would have normally knocked this headache right on out and all I would have needed was some good sleep for 24 hours, that was not the case this time. Remember I told you, this one was different. Well, it gave me a little relief.

I remember going to the Fourth of July fireworks with my mama the next day. But it by no means was gone. It came back stronger than ever. For the next 29 days, I was still in pan. At this point, my parents were scared and concerned; my sister was bringing natural remedies to my house and asking for people to pray for me on social media. Life was just a challenge. I returned back to the emergency room on August 3rd. It was the first day of school for my children so after I saw them off and made sure they weren't worried about me, I drove myself to the hospital. This physician on duty gave me the cocktail again but this time he suggested I speak with neurologist and have an updated RI. Clearly something was wrong, and it needed to be addressed sooner than later. Well after having the MRI, we discovered the problem. There was indeed something wrong. I had excess fluid on the left side of my brain. It was causing problems with my vision and if left untreated, I would definitely lose my vision and who knew what else. I was sitting in the doctor's office with tears in my eyes and as my doctor was speaking, I could see her mouth move but I didn't hear any words coming out.

She gave me a minute to gather myself and once I did, she gave me my options and we picked a treatment plan. Once I left, I cried in the car. I couldn't believe I was back dealing with this. I kept asking why me? I kept asking why was God punishing me? Was I really this awful person that deserved this? All I could do was beg God not to take my vision. See I had already told God while I was waiting for this headache to go away, that I hear Him. Whatever He wanted me to do, I was willing.

It was in this experience I learned that God spoke to me through my health and wellness challenges. I always knew there was a calling on my life, even if I didn't acknowledge it, it's always been there. And it was time to stop running. I had the procedure, drained the fluid and I've been good ever since. God tested my assertion 90 days later in March of 2017. The crossroads had returned and now I had to make a decision. Think about it. First there was the headache, then there was the layoff and coupled with the stress of not being able to find a job in the company that had over 400 positions open was another level of stress that you are never ready for. I was able to keep everything in check that so my headaches wouldn't return but I was definitely walking a tight rope. I've always been the person who would look to my parents for advice and guidance. I would tell them what I was thinking and then boom magically I had the answer. Of course, it wasn't really getting advice from them, it was more so getting confirmation I was on the right track.

I always know when I'm on my own in the decision-making process, when they just listen and never say anything. But surprisingly enough, I didn't need the confirmation this time. I had my ah-ha moment, and the load was lifted off my shoulders. I already had 2 people who said to me I was supposed to be a life coach, so the seed had already been planted. I just didn't put in the time to take it seriously. Many times, when we are facing life changing decisions, the answer is right there before us and always has been. I always said I didn't have time, so now the job was removed and time was not a factor. Not only was the time restraint removed, I also had money coming in so I didn't have to wonder where it was coming from. I now knew what path I should be walking; I became a certified life coach. It was literally a life-changing decision. A decision that has placed me in many rooms and opportunities that I wouldn't have necessarily had if I hadn't kept my word. As you can see, I SURVIVED! I survived and I'm clearer now more than I've ever been that my declaration was necessary.

During this time of uncertainty, I had to depend on my prayer life. I had to depend on my own faith. Although my family was praying, I had to pray for myself. I had to petition God for him to answer me.

And I want to leave you with these 3 things that I learned. 1.God only needs a willing vessel. You don't have to be perfect; you just have to be willing. We run from God and we still expect him to bless us and cover us and keep up with our mess but at what point are you willing to do what it is He's called and created you to do? As my girl MaDonna would say, *"Let me bible it for you." (Romans 8:28KJV) "And we know that all things work together for good to those who love God, to those who are called according to HIS purpose."* My question is do you love God? Are you willing to submit to His will and purpose for your life? Whatever it is that you have been called and created to do, know that all of the things that you have survived were for you to get to this point of walking in His will and purpose for your life.

2.God never left you. We never give it any thought that we aren't alone when we are in the midst of our storms. We think because things aren't going the way we want them to, that God is not hearing us. But in fact, He does. You can rest and shout in the fact that God already know show and when this storm will end. You just have to go through the storm. Need more scripture? Well of course I have it for you. (Matthew 14:22-33 KJV) Remember the story of Peter walking on the water? Well listen, one point we always seem to skip over when we talk about this story is Jesus prayed beforehand. We don't know what Jesus was praying about and praying for, but that prayer went forth. Then when Peter said if it is you, tell me to come to you on the water. Jesus did his part and told Peter to come. Peter is the one who was deviating from the plan. He took his eyes off Jesus and focused on the wrong thing. He let his fears get the best of him. Jesus could have let Peter die, but He didn't. He saved him and told him ye of little faith. Where is your faith? Do you have faith that Jesus will save you? Don't be Peter, be better than Peter. Walk on the water with boldness and know that you are walking to the one who is going to take care of you and not let you die. God is in charge of every single event that takes place in the lives of His children. Aren't you, His child? You have nothing to worry and fear. Feed your faith and starve your fears.

3.You are victorious in every situation because you have God with you. Of course, I got to bible it for you. Deuteronomy 20:4 NIV "For the Lord your God is the one who goes with you to fight for you against your enemies to give you victory." I love this verse because it doesn't say that we have to ask God to go with us; He already does it. So, if He's already there in the battle, what is there to be afraid of? I know the human side of us panics first and prays second but change it around. Pray first and don't panic. Activate your faith and know that the fight is fixed, and you will win. Walk and sleep with the peace of God that is within you. Know that you not only survived, but you got this!

As you continue to read this book, these authors have put together a writing showing the mighty movement of God in their lives and how they survived their different challenges. They are writing chapters and explaining that all is not lost, God is with you. God will order your steps and whatever it is you're dealing with will come to pass. The writers in this book have had to lean on God and pray that He would step in. This too shall pass. Don't get caught up in the present situation that you can't see that. Walk in the authority of who you are and whose you are! You are a King's kid. You too will survive.

She hails from the Big A! Pixie was born and raised in Atlanta, GA and educated in the Cobb County School Systems. She obtained her degree in Accounting and began her entrepreneur journey in 2010 by opening her Accounting and Tax firm. After things slowed down, she returned to Corporate America while still running her firm on a part time basis. After going through a lay off at her job after 2 years, she was at a crossroads in her life. While at this job, 2 of her coworkers spoke to her that she should become a life coach. She's always been the go-to person for advice and had a great listening ear. At time she wasn't sure because she didn't want to go back to school. After sitting still and researching, she found a class and became certified in 1 day. She didn't want to build her business the traditional way so she wrote her first book, "The Power of Purpose." Her book opened doors and connected her with people who have been instrumental in assisting her to build a life coaching business. Tapping into her write skills, she became a ghost writer. In 2020, she released her second book, Forgiveness is key and started her publishing company. She published her first collaboration project as well titled "An Anchor for the Ages." It's her goal to publish 50 new black authors. Pixie lives by the mantra "If she takes care of God's people, God will take care of her".

No Longer The Shadow

Deborah A. Franklin

As a woman walking with her head held high unapologetically smart, black, fierce, and intelligent, one would think she has it all together. She doesn't have a worry in the world. She has her stuff together and has achieved all her dreams. Well, that is what I wanted everyone to believe. I was a walking, breathing shell of a person, who was so shattered and broken within.

Living a lie is hard work especially when you're fighting through low self-esteem and feelings of rejection. Yes, that person was me. I had achieved what looks good in public: the degrees, jobs, and cars, but I was not whole. All of these were material things, but I didn't know love. Honestly, I didn't know how to love myself. I threw myself into everything for others and neglected myself on so many levels.

Shattered pieces of a person scattered in many different directions. I struggled with relationships because I didn't know how to have a relationship with myself. I have shared this story so many times, but it goes without saying I didn't have a voice to speak up for myself, because I had it snuffed out throughout the years.

I recently had a friend to tell me that I really got on her nerves, because I never spoke up for myself or didn't fight for what I knew was right. In her observations she noticed that I would shut down and retreat. I wouldn't say anything but would cut those persons off. Yes, she was entirely correct. What she didn't know was that I had suffered so much verbal abuse as a child and adult that I all knew was to retreat and figure out how to protect myself. So, if that meant going into my cave and hibernating, then that would be just what I did. This is what began my journey of living in the shadows. I was operating as a ghost. Doing things for others and never getting credit was all good for me. Always the cheerleader, but never the quarterback was an easy position to play. This allowed me not to have to deal with rejection or acceptance. I was just a shell of a person. The crazy part about all of this, no one knew. I would still attempt to do things, but it was carefully done under the auspices of ministry. I could try things under the radar. If it worked, all good, but if it failed, for the most part, I would get well, you can try again. I found my safety zone.

As I continued to live my life in the shadows of others, family, ministry, friends, etc. I built a wall around me. When I look back, God was setting me up for where I am now. I never had support from people I thought would have my back. I soon learned I was special. I could never be the one who could ride someone else's coat tail to make it. I would have to work extra hard because I had certain standards. But most of all, I had to learn to trust God with everything. I learned that everything I did was a But God experience.

As I continued to come into myself and slowly learning that I was smart enough and good enough to be a strong leader, it was a hard road. Again, on the outside I was wearing the avatar of confidence but shattered in so many pieces on the inside. I strongly remember going to a service and the prophet speaking over me that I needed to deal with the little girl on the inside. I had to forgive her and let her know that she was able to be successful. I had to let her know that she was worthy to reach higher levels in life.

This was hard work. To have to go back into the depts of my memory and deal with all the verbal hurt that I had suffered from others, that I eventually began to inflict upon myself. The darkness that I felt over me was draining and felt like shattered glass shards in my hands, arms and on the bottom of my feet. I was in so much pain. I had to do the work to heal the pain. Yes, I have the scars, but I learned that all the pieces of me that looked shattered all over the place were beautiful colored glass that represented all I went through, but now healed from were coming together to make a beautiful mosaic. That had value and sturdy to withstand anything that would come to me.

This mosaic that you see today has withstood so many storms in life, but I am here standing strong and ready to take on the world. I am no longer worried about what others may say about me. Do I still hear those negative voices in my head? Absolutely. But now I know how to deal with them. I know how to cast those feeling right back to the pits of hell from whence they came. I have embarrassed who I truly am. I am ready to take on the world and live the life I was intended to live. Every colored piece of glass in this mosaic has a meaning and tells the story of how I'm an overcomer and more than ready to take on the world, unapologetically me.

Deborah A. Franklin is the Founder/CEO of Conversations Entertainment Group that is the corporate headquarters for Deborah Franklin Publishing and Church Girl CEO. With over 20 years in the entertainment and education industry she has the knowledge and expertise to assist you to catapult your career to the next level.

Deborah Franklin also has a heart for women to expand their mindsets pass what they can see and not to be afraid to tell their stories to the world. As a survivor of verbal abuse, she has learned to rise above what has been said to her and about her to be the authentic representative of who she was created to be.

Deborah Franklin is the author of 'adjectives,' '21 Days 21 Minutes of Prayer & Meditation,' '#5 30 Days of Motivation & Inspiration' and 'The Prayer of Jabez in the Marketplace'; host of

Conversations w/Deborah Franklin and a media coach. Deborah has been working as a media coach for several years with clients who are authors, speakers and entertainers.

Deborah also uses her platform to give other aspiring artist and outlet to let their talents shine. Her ultimate goal in life is to help others to ignite the power within to propel them to their destiny while walking in their purpose.

Take It All, But Not My Baby!

Chiara Noble

I was standing in the courtroom anxious, nervous, and angry. I can't even say which of the these outweighed the other because they all melded into one fireball of rollercoaster emotions I had been wrestling with for months. I glanced over at my ex and his wife, who sat at the opposing side with his attorney and wondered many things; but at the forefront of my mind was how I was ready, confident even, for this series of unfortunate events to end with me as the victor.

My black skirt suit was pressed to perfection, complimented with a white blouse underneath, and I wore conservative black pumps and sheer hose. Being administrative, organized, and meticulous by nature, I thought for sure that I was prepared and that I could do things on my own without an attorney, so I didn't have a lawyer, but I surely looked like one. I had prayed, fasted, enlisted prayer warriors and memorized scriptures. I had my mom with me, and I was ready for battle. More than likely, it would be the most important battle of my life – custody of my child, my first-born son.

The proceedings began. Because I was self-representing, I had no idea of what was to come. It didn't matter how intelligent, well-dressed and well-spoken I was. The court didn't care about any of that. Here I was, a single, pregnant woman (by a different man) standing up against a married couple who seemingly had it all together.

The opposing side's attorney went first and aimed right for my jugular. She dragged my name and character up and down through the mud and back again. I was involved in a modeling group, and I had posted some risqué photos on the digital platform, MySpace. There were also photos of me at different clubs and social events prior to my current pregnancy. They used my social media as a weapon, and it worked. Not only did they obtain and use information from my personal pages, but they scanned and scoured friends of friend's pages, submitting photographs and evidence to the court that I was not only an unfit mother, but that I exercised poor judgment. They even had screenshots of posts where I referred to or referenced people as friends, then showed pictures of those same people in unsavory settings. Every objection that I attempted to make was overruled. Statements I made were twisted around, and I was given no opportunity to clarify.

I was done before I even really began.

You ever seen those TV shows or movies where the lawyer was so good that they caused the person testifying to become confused, stuttering and stumbling over words and eventually fall apart? That was me, and I didn't stand a chance.

Defending those social media posts fell on deaf ears. I wasn't swift enough to counter this destruction of my character. My mind was screaming, but all of my thoughts were lodged in my throat! How could I attempt to convince the court that I had changed? That I was now leading a very simple, yet boring life? That no matter what this evidence looked like, that I loved my son and would literally lay down and die for him?

There was nothing I could do. I made the terrible mistake of thinking that as his mother, the woman who birthed him, who spent twenty-three hours in labor, would have given me the greatest advantage. I banked on the court automatically awarding custody to me, a hard-working, upstanding citizen. But after my ex's attorney got through with me, in an instant, I was made to feel and look like trash.

I sat there grasping onto what was left of my faith, my sanity, and my last meal! I felt nauseated and gripped the side of the table until my knuckles turned white. I couldn't even look his way because

I didn't want him to see me mentally crumbling, about to lose it. I was hyperventilating, as I was holding on by a slippery thread. I simply could not fathom that the court's decision would result in losing my son.

As I awaited the verdict, the history with my ex flashed through my mind. If I had known then what I know now, I would have done things differently. It was August of 2007 and my son was 5 years old. Reflecting on the day that everything spiraled out of control, I remember saying the words to my son's father, "I will see you in court." It was after many years of arguing, harassment, among many other challenges that I became fed up. That phone conversation -- those six words -- I wish I could take back. Sometimes I wonder if I had not said them out loud and kept them to myself how much different the outcome would have been. A word of advice to anyone who is going through a custody battle: never let the other person know what your intentions are! Wait, even before that, try to resolve your issues outside of the court. I cannot emphasize this enough! Do everything humanly possible to stay out of the court system. You do not want a judge or magistrate dictating when, where, and how you can see your child and how much each month that child is worth.

In my case, court was the only option I had, so I filed paperwork. Up until that point, we had a verbal agreement of shared custody, but after I filed the paperwork, I spent the next three months being denied visits with my son. Our verbal agreement we had in place went out the window. (Later he admitted in court to keeping him from me for the three months, claiming he was afraid I would keep him and not give him back.)

During those three months, I called, texted, e-mailed and called the police multiple times and was still refused access to my son. Now I don't know about you but going from a day or two to three months seemed like an eternity. And the police really can't help you in situations like this. They are limited as to how far they can go where domestic situations are concerned, especially without a court order and even then, there can be issues.

To compound matters, my ex had also filed paperwork *two days* before I did. Because of that, his paperwork took the lead. Two days changed the sequence of events. In the end, the result was a temporary court order was issued in November of 2007. We were to have shared custody but by default, he had primary physical custody because guess what? He and his wife enrolled him in school in the midst of all this. So because he was enrolled in school with his father's physical address, residency with him was established.

In retrospect, that was a "snake in the grass" move. I believe he was advised to do this and unfortunately, I underestimated the extent he would go through to hurt me at my core. I thought because we had an agreement for me to be able to see my son Monday, Wednesday, Thursday and every other weekend, it would be okay. NOT!!

As if him getting his way wasn't enough, a few months later I received the next set of court papers, which was a modification of his previously filed papers. It had the most absurd allegations! It said that I was drinking, smoking marijuana and transporting my child without a car seat. We went before a Master in court, not a judge. This was another tough life lesson. Do not go this route if you can avoid it. The Master or Magistrate is a low-level judge who can only make recommendations, not issue court orders. If you are going this route alone with no attorney, after the Master's recommendation, you have to pretty much put it into correct form yourself and file it with the court, then wait for a judge to sign-off on it and make it an order -- all of which costs! The Master heard all testimony and made her recommendation, that I was granted primary physical custody and child support, and he was to have visitation. The only major stipulation was that our son was to finish out the reminder of the school year at the school they had him enrolled in until the end of the year.

Yes! Victory! I did it, I won...or so I thought. The next thing I received were exceptions to the Master's recommendation, from an attorney that he hired, followed by more accusations of me having unstable housing and my father being an active drug user, living in the home. Oh, and last but certainly not least, it was stated that I *relinquished custody to him*. What nonsense!

My mind snapped back to present day and the verdict. God, please do not rip my heart out. Please do not allow him to win.

As the judge awarded primary physical custody to my ex-husband and his wife, I was frozen. Although I was granted joint legal custody with visitation, it just was not the same. I was also then ordered to pay them child support. Yes, whoever has primary physical custody gets awarded child support. As the judge banged the gavel and said, "Court adjourned," I just stood there. I could not move. I couldn't breathe. I was dizzy, sweaty and my vision blurred. For what felt like an eternity but in essence was probably sixty seconds, I was totally distraught and incoherent. As I began to come to the realization of what had just happened, immense sadness and dread began to set in. I grabbed my bag and ran from the courtroom, almost tripping down the hall to the closest restroom I could find. It was a three-stall bathroom but no one else was inside, not that it would have mattered anyway. Nothing mattered in that moment. I began to cry and scream hysterically. I'm sure that I could be heard clear down the hallway. I cried so hard—harder than I probably ever had. I could feel my stomach start to cramp and, in an instant, I was vomiting. It was then that I heard knocking on the door. At first, I thought someone was knocking on the outside of the bathroom door from the hallway, but as I wiped my mouth and blew my nose, I looked down and saw shoes. It was then that I heard a voice say, "Ms. Greene, are you okay? Can we talk?"

I flushed the toilet, blew my nose again and slowly opened the door and on the other side was the same woman who destroyed me. It was my son's father's attorney. I glared at her as I exited the stall to wash my hands and my face. She continued speaking. She told me that she was sorry. In the moment I thought to myself *you're sorry?!* I wanted to scream at her and say all sorts of hateful things. I wanted to ask if she had children, and even if she didn't, how could ANY woman take away another woman's child with a clear conscience? I was certain I wasn't the first and probably wouldn't be the last. Instead I glared at her, opened the bathroom door and almost bumped into my mom who took one look at the attorney and simply said to her, "Please leave my daughter be." We exited the courthouse, and I spent the remainder of that day and many other days in agony, but I survived.

If It had not been for the support system that I had in place, which at the time was my mother, brother, and a few close friends, I surely would have lost my mind. It sounds cliché, but I tell people to this day if it had not been for God's grace and mercy, I truly would not have made it out alive. I never thought about taking my own life but had dreams and visions of being taken away from this place so that I didn't have to suffer anymore. I attended church regularly and prayed often, and I know that it was nothing but God that brought me through. He surrounded me with just the right people to help.

You may think my faith would have been shaken or even tossed aside, but it only brought me closer to Him. I have been emotionally and mentally scarred from this ordeal but thank God I don't look like what I've been through! I will say that looking back, I should have gone to counseling because here I am all these years later, damaged, but it's okay! I have been married for almost 10 years to a wonderful man who ironically, I met at a nightclub in 2008, the same night that I decided clubbing wasn't for me anymore. He is my better half, my voice of reason. We are equally yoked. We are raising our middle child, who I was pregnant with in my story, and our youngest child together. We also are co-raising (along with her mom and stepfather) his eleven-year-old daughter, my bonus baby. I am living a happy life, one that I have always dreamed of for myself but never thought it would happen.

My past does not define me, nor did it destroy me. All the nights that I spent hugging my tear-soaked pillow after pacing the halls walking past my son's bedroom, smelling his clothes and sleeping with his stuffed animals, are a thing of the past. To this day, my son is still not in my life. I have rarely seen him since that day in court, 12 years ago. I want nothing more but than to have a healthy, stable and nurturing relationship with him but the events *after court* leading up until today have so far prevented that from happening.

As I tell people all the time, God's timing is His own, but it is perfect. I was not always in this headspace. It is only recently that I have been able to tell my story to a select few and share parts of it with people that I felt needed to hear it. I had so much shame, and I was so worried about what people would think of me. There is so much more that happened, but it's for another time.

Please be careful with social media accounts. My social media these days are an accurate reflection of who I am, but it wasn't always. I know you may be reading this and saying, "I will post, say and share what I want on MY page," but please don't. People are out here literally losing everything every day for what they chose to share with the public. Some things are meant to be kept not necessarily secret, but private. Prospective employers also scan your social media accounts too.

If you are facing a custody battle, my wish for you, my takeaway, is please don't just assume custody is given to the mother automatically. As you can see from my story, no matter how good you look or present yourself, never assume anything! I later learned that there are resources, such as the pro bono resource center and in my state, the Maryland volunteer law service where there are people to help you through this process. There is also legal aid that has attorneys you can obtain for free or for low cost, that charge according to your income. There is help out there! Don't you dare try to go at this alone. I want to close by saying don't make the same mistakes I did, because I believe in this life, everything happens for a reason. If I can survive and live to tell the story, by His grace, you can too.

Chiara A. Noble is a visionary, a woman of many talents who wears many hats. She is an ordained minister, wife, mother, daughter, sister. Many people call her friend. She is a Property Manager by profession, newly published author and co-host of Victory Talk, a virtual talk show centered around helping people to grow, speak and live a victorious life.

"Key", as her family and close friends call her, is a woman after God's own heart. One who desires to help people from all walks of life to get motivated and to stay the course. She has faced many personal trials and tribulations over the course of the years but lives by the saying "storms make trees take deeper roots." Those people, places and things have helped to mold and shape her into the woman that she is today, and she wouldn't trade that for anything.

Chiara along with her husband Me'Sean, serve on the ministerial staff at Victorious Living Faith

Ministries, under the leadership of Pastor Phillip A. Miller. She is both dedicated and passionate about bringing people to Christ and helping the lost return to the fold. She currently serves as the Pastor's assistant and the Have a Heart to Help Ministry, which works diligently to assist the homeless and underprivileged communities from Harford County to Baltimore City and everywhere in between.

Chiara was born and raised in Baltimore, so she recognizes and understands the needs of the people in the community. Her desire is to help people to heal from the inside out. Children are near and dear to her heart, and personal experiences have steered her towards her future career plans. Those include returning to school to complete her degree in Behavioral Psychology, and she desires to work for, or open, a private practice geared toward treating adolescents.

In her spare time, Chiara likes to draw, paint, write and sing. What she loves most is spending time with her family and close friends and just enjoying every moment that life has to offer.

CONTACT: Chiara "Key" Noble:

On the web: http://Vlfminstrys.org/

Facebook: https://www.facebook.com/chiara.noble.1

Twitter: @Keybaby81
Instagram: Keybaby81/ Chiara Noble
Email: chiara.noble@vlfministrys.org

My mission in life is not merely to survive, but to thrive; and to do so with some passion, some compassion, some humor, and some style. -Maya Angelou

Healing From The Inside Out

MaDonna Williams

Life throws you curve balls when you least expect them. Sometimes they are direct and in your face. Other times, they are subtle little nudges trying to get your attention. If you are a person of faith, you better believe that God is always in the mix.

During a routine examination with my primary care physician, when she checked my breasts, she asked me had I ever felt anything odd. I was like, "No," but clearly she wasn't happy with the findings of her examination, and I honestly didn't think anything of it. She insisted I go and get all of these additional exams and I was like, "I don't have time for this."

You have to understand at that point, I was last in my life. I had four kids at home who needed me, and a husband, and I needed to work. All of these "tests" sounded like a waste of time, taking me away from my very hectic routine, none of which included me being Number One. But at the doctor's urging, I went ahead with the next steps.

After they did the mammogram and ultrasound, they needed to run some other tests. I vaguely remember them talking about polyps or cysts or something. I was already stressed the heck out, trying to be the best mother, wife, church member, employee, friend, daughter, and so on. I was trying to live my best life *for everybody else,* and all of these tests were interrupting my flow. *Why couldn't these medical professionals see that?*

They wanted to do a biopsy. I remember thinking, "Look, I need to go run payroll and you trying to hold me up!" Yes, everything was before my health. I was on autopilot for years, tending to everybody and their mama but not myself.

I shared these details with my cousin who insisted I follow through, so under duress, I went and did the biopsy and just waited for the results. When the phone call came through, I was at work. Noticing the phone number, I closed my office door and answered the call.

The nurse on the other end, after confirming who I was, said bluntly, "You have disease in both of your breasts."

Now what did she say? Disease?? Dis/ease. This was a prophetic revelation. But at the time, I couldn't even process that. And when she delivered this life-changing news, there was no softening in her tone, no "please sit down," not even a warning. It was a gut-punch and up to that point, you could say I was used to that kind of verbal assault.

I flatly responded, "Okay, what do I need to do?"

I ended up going in for a consultation. She shared what my options were with a big old book of resources and information. It was like breast cancer university. I really was in such denial, until they used the term "breast cancer" and as life would have it, it was in both breasts.

I held on to this news, not really trying to tell anyone anything. It was part of that "home training" I received: *What happens in this house, stays in this house.* So I suffered in silence for a long time with this diagnosis and put it in a mental lock box along with several other secrets.

I was strong, let me tell you, going about my daily life like this was no big deal. It was my coping mechanism to pretend all was right with the world. But right before surgery, I felt grief come over me. I looked at my husband and I told him, "I'm about to cry." I had not shed one tear until that point, but slowly but surely, my emotions were starting to get the best of me.

At the age of 42, I had to have both breasts removed. Afterwards, the doctor wanted to know what kind of pills did I want, but I refused. I decided I wanted to determine how I got to this point and holistically heal myself on my own. I did work with a plastic surgeon for reconstruction. On my last visit to see the plastic surgeon, when the stitches were removed, there was a space, like a hole.

I asked, "What's this hole?"

His answer was profound, but I'm sure he didn't know the impact it had on me. I'm sure he had said this statement to many women time and time again and no doubt, it was taken with a grain of salt.

His response was: "You're going to have to heal from the inside out."

A neon light bulb went on, an "ah-ha" moment. He was a doctor, but God was using him to send me a message.

Healing from the inside out.

Perhaps you've heard that stress can kill you. Walking around constantly with anger in your heart, along with bitterness, worry, pain, anxiety, depression, and unforgiveness will eat you alive. It can shorten your lifespan by several years, causing you to have high blood pressure, heart problems, and sleep deprivation among other diseases.

I don't know why at my young age I had cancer in both breasts, but I can tell you I had a lot of years of built up junk in the attic so much so, you would have needed a flashlight to navigate through all of the dark crevices of my mind. I was bitter, jealous and envious and it trickled into anger.

There was a lot of dis/ease in my life. A lot of uneasiness that I kept buried, suppressed in the depths of my soul because facing them would mean I would have to admit that my well-put together outside did not match my damaged insides, that the persona that I showed every day was a mere shell of what was really going on underneath.

When he said those words, I had a flashback to being married at an early age to my first husband. I've been a Christian all my life, and I felt that God had prepared me to be young and married. I met my first husband at the singles' ministry in church, which should have meant that we were equally yoked, had the same values and shared the same hopes and dreams for our future. The icing on the cake was he was a single father with custody of his infant daughter. I found that to be very admirable.

We had an idyllic wedding – I mean all the bells and whistles. He had a lot of money from a cash settlement, so no expense was spared. We honeymooned in the Caribbean. It was also my first plane flight, and I loved everything about it. I remember us snorkeling in crystal blue waters and how beautiful our accommodations were. The weather was gorgeous, and everything was picture perfect. Not even a week into our stay, I was in the bathroom and then something set him off. I don't really know if it was something I said or did, but next thing I knew, I was being pummeled by his fists, so much so, I was on the floor. Bodily fluids had escaped and pooled around me as he stood over me.

I can't remember him being sorry. It was like something came over him and in a matter of minutes, I became a statistic, a battered wife. There were visible bruises that lingered and remained not only on the outside, but emotionally. I found out later he suffered from seizures that affected his mood and would cause him to "go off" the deep end and lash out in violent ways. I was at the receiving end more times than I care to admit, but this was not something I openly shared with anybody, and I endured his abuse for the sake of our marriage; for the sake of our kids, because he had purchased my childhood home for us, and I wanted to make it our home, although years later, he legally prevented me from entering the house…ever! And this was just the tip of the iceberg.

Sitting in that doctor's office caused a flood of memories and incidents that had been eating away at my very soul. I knew I had to go back and heal and forgive myself, forgive my parents, stepparents, my husband, my ex-husband, my children. I did a lot of reading and self-help to help me heal from the inside. It really put me on a path of enlightenment about bitterness. God walked me through that journey.

As they say, your story is not for you but it's for someone else. My first husband passed away, but what I went through was certainly not in vain. I'm committed to helping women of faith break free from anger and bitterness to discover their true identity so I founded Treasure Your Inner Beauty.

My business, Treasure Your Inner Beauty, helps high achieving women of faith break free from mental and emotional struggles that have kept them from living their authentic life. They spend their lives hiding behind material things, that shimmery outer cloak, showing only what they want people to see, while what is going on inside is nothing but turmoil because they are too proud to let anyone know they've made mistakes, the marriage is a wreck, the bills are not paid, they hate their job, they feel ugly and have been abused, or are simply being held together with tissue paper, disintegrating by the second.

I'm here for the woman of faith who is afraid to let her guard down because of what society says, what family might think, or they've been living up to everyone else's expectations that don't truly align with their divine appointment.

What is needed and what I offer is a total shift in mindset, a transformation of the heart.

Being afraid to really be who you are called to be is nothing but a bad seed that has been watered over time. You may have been told certain things and have held on to certain beliefs that have settled in your soul, and you wrestle with whether or not they are true. Those negative seeds were watered and then germinated within you and became toxic to the point of taking precedence over your life.

I'm speaking from experience. I had a whole lot of seeds of bitterness that started to eat away at me from the inside out. Until I went through that cancer diagnosis and surgery, I was in denial about how those things I held to – stored up in my internal greenhouse – had become spiny thorns that were tearing away at my very existence. In addition to dealing with heartache from my past, I had many labels placed upon me such as big mouth, mean girl, smart-aleck, and other unsavory tags that fertilized those bitterness seeds. I had to do a deep examination of not only the HOW but the WHY related to me getting to that point. Through consistent prayer, intentional reading, and studying the Word, God revealed to me that the way to be free was to actually kill each negative entity from the root and replace it with God's forgiveness and love. Coming to terms with your past and how it affects your day-to-day life is a major step towards healing.

When you hold on to bitterness, anger, envy and other negative energy, it will manifest itself through many ways such as sickness, insomnia, distractions, short-temper, isolation, depression, stress and many other ailments...like cancer!

When we work together, I'm looking to uncover and release the real YOU. I'm coming to blow your whole house down. Your stoic outer layer of perceived impenetrable brick will become a pile of straw as we work together to reveal those inner feelings that are truly holding you back from achieving your divine greatness. I leave you with this reflection from Jim Rohn from his book, "The Five Major Pieces to the Life Puzzle." I pray it speaks to your soul:

- What we think determines what we believe
- What we believe influences what we choose
- What we choose defines what we are
- What we are attracts what we have.

If you are a woman of faith, I want to work with you on planting the right seeds in order to produce a fruitful harvest, while also learning how to block out noise that would try to steal your peace. If I was able to persevere, you can too.

 **MaDonna Williams** is a passionate mindset coach who helps Successful Women of Faith who feel broken within to reclaim fulfillment and inner healing in 6 weeks by teaching them how to treasure their inner beauty.

Each woman's journey is unique and can be filled with emotional and traumatic experiences. With specialized support, MaDonna personally accompanies women to overcome any roadblocks or circumstances by building destiny bridges of where they are now to where they want to be. The end result is freedom and a pathway for them to create their own legacy for future generations.

After years of providing for and supporting others (including her eight children), a breast cancer diagnosis reminded her of her grandmother's words: "Don't just exist. LIVE!"

MaDonna's personal journey of self-rediscovery and living commenced in answering a spiritual calling and becoming a certified mindset coach so she could help restore other women on their journey of finding their purpose and leaving a legacy.

In addition to her mindset coaching business, MaDonna is an electrifying singer, published author, inspirational speaker and loves to garden while being assisted by her sidekick cat named Shadow.

Join her live each Saturday on YouTube @ MaDonna.INcourage for more ways on living your fulfilled life, or on Instagram: IG MaDonnaINcourage. Remember, don't just tolerate your life, enjoy your life.

It's More Than Just a Journey

Delphia Sheila Marshall

I'm resting right now, surrounded by lavender scented bubbles, in a hot soaking tub praising God for this moment in time where I can take a few minutes to pour some golden nuggets into you of encouragement, resilience and faith. Whatever you are going through, it's just a journey; trust and believe you will pass through it. You will make it out. You are born to survive. Sometimes it can be difficult, but you are an overcomer. Say it out loud, **I AM A SURVIVOR!** Every now and then, you have to talk to yourself, sow into your own life and then wait on God for the answer. He will whisper it to you or show you a sign.

Let me tell you, I speak from a personal space. We go through stuff all the time. Some journeys are more difficult than others, but with each hurdle, we are building character and mental toughness along the way.

Why don't you grab your favorite drink and sit with me for a while as I tell you a little bit about how not heeding those early warning signs of dysfunction can lead to decades of heartache and disappointment.

I've been married twice, but the first time was a test run, you know, it sounded good and it looked good, but I wasn't ready. But when you're in your early twenties, shoot, you think you know everything.

When I was younger, we were in church all the time. It was a good thing, because it kept me off those streets. I really loved the church we were at, and I even met my second husband, "Charles," but my crystal ball was broken at the time, and Charles didn't come until later.

Before Charles was "Lenny." He was cute and popular, so I dated him. We moved into this really cute apartment in Baltimore, and it was my first time living on my own and also my first time away from home. My father hated that I did that. I was a daddy's girl. My father's name was Herbert and that's what we called him too – not daddy. Let me tell you, Herbert brought me a brand spanking new 1972 white-on-white fully loaded Mercury Cougar. Yup, loved that car; drove it until the doors fell off. When I would come outside to leave for work, my car would be GONE. No need to panic, though; I knew Herbert came and removed it. That was his way of letting me know he did not approve of my decision, cause y'all know back then, adults didn't know how to talk to us about life. In slavery, folks didn't talk much either; they sung, if they needed to say something…or they just rolled up and stole your ride in the middle of the night!

Well, after me and Lenny "shacked up," next thing I knew we were getting married. I was 22 when I married and with child in my belly at 23. During the marriage, I gave birth to Kalyan, our son. We divorced soon after. We were just too darn young. He was actually a good husband -- not so good a father. Left me to raise a boy on my own. Not only that, he enjoyed the streets and was into smoking and other stuff, and that was not me. Discovered he had a chick on the side while I was pregnant. Did I say he was a good husband? Scratch that thought. I was like why would a sister break the *sister code*, dating *my* married man (Lenny) who was about to be a father? She tormented me constantly – the mere existence of her was a thorn in my side. Because of his betrayal, I couldn't share the same space with Lenny, so I moved back home to my parents for a minute.

 Fast forward 17 years later, and I was at the dry cleaners one day. Some cleaners have a bulletin board to share events. Posted on the board was a flyer announcing the opening of church nearby. I jotted down the information, went home immediately and called to see if it could be my new church home. When I called, the Pastor actually answered the phone and we chatted a good while. I was amazed. I never had that type of communication with a *Man of The Cloth*. That was over 29 years ago. I am still there, New Faith Blessed Church, MD (NFBC). But the wow factor here is when I went back to the cleaners to use their services...are you ready? There was no cleaners. I cannot explain it. You can make it out how you wish.

At this point in my life, I had a teenage son and just purchased my first brand new townhouse. Moved in with just my belongings in green trash bags. Today, I need those trash bags to purge my home. I'm about to be a contestant for the TV show, "Hoarders!" I have too much stuff. Need boxes now, not bags, and people to help. You available? God is good!

Okay, back to the story. So I'm single, loving life, and then POW. One day at NFBC singles' ministry, a friend brought Charles to our meeting. Yes, that same Charles from when I was younger. There was this lady in attendance of our ministry meeting that was very much interested in meeting/dating Charles. This lady often invited him to do things, but I think he was saying no. I can't mention her name or anything to give you clues; she is still angry 29 years later. When I see her now, there is fire in her eyes. She used to call and tell me what she was going to do to attract him. At this point, I had zero interest in him, but he had 100% interest in me. I wanted to stay single for a minute, but my friend called me and said she had him on the other line, then said "Y'all, I have to go, continue talking." Now who said I wanted to do this three-way? But I was roped in and accepted the invitation.

Of course, one of the first things out of my mouth was about the other lady. He assured me there was no interest on his part. After a few more interactions, next thing I knew, we were dating. We actually met and married within one year. I know, I know...

He proposed with the most beautiful diamond ring during dinner. I still have it, been thinking about pawning it, but I like it, so I wear it sometimes as jewelry.

Here is where the idea of marriage, love and happiness comes into play and how the desire for a perfect union can cloud your judgment, or because your sister-friend hooked you up, you start to believe what is before you must be God-ordained. All of this causes you to make wrong decisions, often times, over and over again, even though there may be neon warning signs blinking like a strobe light.

I recall the evening before my marriage to Charles. I was shown several signs of why I should have called off the wedding. I remember the evening like it was yesterday. We had a house full of folks, helping us prepare for the wedding. I went down to the lower level where Charles was and found him on his knees scrubbing the floor, preparing for company. I called out to him "Charles," and he did not answer. I continued to call out. He never stopped scrubbing; he was moving like a possessed person, just moving that rag in a continuous fast motion in a circle. It was as if he could not stop if he wanted, so very robotic, indicating no life throughout the process. He just scrubbed that same spot, never acknowledging my presence. At that point, I was like *what the heck*? My brain started revealing information: *lady you need to run, this is not normal.*

Thinking back, he was showing signs of mental illness. I did not know it. I thought about calling the marriage ceremony off, but what would the people say? You know how we don't want our business in the streets. Don't want to be shamed. I cared more about that than what the Holy Spirit was saying to me at the time. I chose to walk around with my eyes wide shut, knowing something was not right.

At first, it was to be a small ceremony in the Pastor's office. Once Pastor reminded us that we needed witnesses, the event grew to having all the bells and whistles.

At this point, we were "knee deep" in it, so I proceeded on, only to be released from the marriage 20+ years later. Our honeymoon cruise shed a lot of light on what was to come. For example, almost immediately, he came down with the sniffles, you know, like allergy symptoms. He stayed "sick" the entire time. He literally shut down and stopped participating in any of the cruise events both on and off the ship. He stopped communicating and became mute towards me. Believe me, I tried to crack that shell but just like him being in a zone when scrubbing that floor, there was an invisible forcefield blocking me out. We were like two married strangers on our honeymoon. I dealt with it and got through it, more like prayed my way through it, and our honeymoon was cut short.

That prayer time was worshipping time for me, and I relied on it often. I recall the First Lady telling me, "Just because a person carries a Bible don't make him saved." Whew chile...she was correct.

He never wanted to do anything or go anywhere but home, down in the lower level on his computer. That was the other mistress that I knew about – his computer. What was on it, I wondered, that demanded his attention? I would find myself upstairs watching TV or at church. We did this dance and over time we, drifted apart as partners, and weeks turned into months, then months turned into 20+ years.

But there was yet another intrusion, in addition to the computer mistress, that appeared without warning and rocked my world.

Out of the blue, I received a call from the bank that someone in a casino in Las Vegas was consistently withdrawing money from my account. I did not even know Charles was in Las Vegas, can't recall where I thought he was. Next thing I knew, Charles was calling.

After barely a *hello*, this is what he said: "You want me to come home or go to my mother?"

This was a surreal moment for me but also an eye-opener. It was in that moment I discovered he was a gambler. Sadly, I had no clue. All the bills were paid on time, so I had no reason to question our finances.

That call with him asking should he go home to his mommy told me he was probably afraid of my response, which he should have been. I asked him to come home and explain to me how he planned to return my money to the tune of several thousand dollars. By the way, I'm still waiting for that refund.

Addictions come in all forms, not just drugs. This was yet another sign of what was to come but what did I do? I stayed in the marriage. Because of what we accumulated together, I had convinced myself it actually was a good marriage, but it wasn't. To some, it's embarrassing to be divorced. I was one of the "some" at the time. Folks weathered the storm all the time and you tell yourself this, too, can be fixed. Not! He was a gambler deep down in his soul. He played craps (dice) and poker. He was out of control and not recognizing the demon, so I had to protect myself and my assets. We had joint accounts, but that became a done deal.

I stayed resilient through the end. Even with all of his gambling antics and obvious mental afflictions, we moved into a newly built custom home. You can say the *dream home*. But as they say: a house does not make a home.

Massive change had definitely crept into our relationship. The bouts of non-communication became the norm and went on for long periods of time. Church was over for Charles. He would go to his space, and I would go to mine.

Things stayed unworkable for years. What became obvious to me was he was sick, suffering from some sort of health problem – maybe both mental and physical. His breath was so strong and sour, I would tell him about it. He just got upset and went into denial. I recall one day, I looked in the medicine cabinet that he used and *Lord Jesus*, it was so much prescription drugs that he was actively taking, I wanted to cry. He was overdosing on prescription drugs. (My observation.) When I asked about it, I would get laid out in a foreign language. I laid low after that. If he wanted to go toe-to-toe, I kept my tongue in my mouth and my side-eye working. I was at war with demons.

I made a conscious decision that my sanity was worth more than my materialistic things. It was okay to leave it behind. Pick your battles, and don't fight when you can make peace. God will fight for you; go to Him. (Deuteronomy 3:22, NASB). Whether we are resisting temptation or battling fear, God has promised to fight with and for us, as we place our hope and confidence in Him. And when you read scripture, read the entire chapter so you can get the full flavor. Then go back and reflect on the particular verses. That's what I did.

One day Charles left the house and never came back. He did the same thing to his daughter's mother – left out one day and never came back. Never said a word, no note, no voicemail, morse code, carrier pigeon, nothing! I thought I was different, special. I thought that wouldn't happen to me not because I was better, but because I was too smart to get caught up in some mess like that, but love is indeed blind. And the sting of a second divorce sounded like failure before my family, before God, and for myself. Divorce meant I had to leave my dream house and start all over again on my own. I knew I was capable of breaking free, but still, the severing of what was left a stain.

When a union ends, it's easy to get depressed, feel inadequate, wondering what else you could have done to save it. But you must stay healthy when you are experiencing trials and tribulations. When we allow our health to fail, there goes our strength. If you have energy, faith, and a strong support system, you can conquer all. It's important to stay healthy as you emerge into and out of this journey. You should get into what I call, Survivor Mode. Here are some tips for taking care of YOU. Always take care of yourself first.

Survivor Mode

- Eat right. Ditch the sugar, it's not good for you. Read food labels for sugar and carb intakes. For me, I am loving unsweet tea with lemons and crushed ice.
- Try the air-fryer. Jesus! I took the plunge and purchased a toaster air fryer. Worth every dime and then some.
- Pre Covid-19, I would have said to join a gym, but with social distancing, try walking instead, as much as you can. I am a walker and love it. I am not a cute walker; I just get dressed and out the door normally in the morning. I walk about 5 miles; my minimum is 3 miles in the morning. The walk gives me clarity. The fresh air is amazing. Walking in the rain sometimes

is so serene. And if it's snowing, it's so beautiful to walk through. A sports medicine doctor told me to *focus on strength, motion, flexibility* and said, *mainly the kitchen is your enemy.* Did y'all in the back hear that? That kitchen can be your health's best friend or worst enemy.
- My pride and joy, the bubble bath. I take them often. There is nothing like some warm water, essential oils, Epsom salt (remember I work out), and bubble bath foam. I get the best ideas and thoughts in the bubble bath. Try it!
- Get plenty of sleep. Now this is a good one also. Whatever room you make as your bedroom or where you sleep, design it for comfort. A good night's sleep is important. You want to create an oasis retreat.

No matter where you are in life, these tips can be a jumpstart towards a new and

improved you.

I'm still traveling through the broken marriage. Sometimes you have to be silent. Time to **Re-Set** and **Rebrand** yourself. Pray not because you need a particular thing, but just say *"THANK YOU LORD."*

At the end of the day, marriage is not easy. It's work. You have to have something in your marriage that drives you, makes you want to jump up and make waffles. Something that makes you want to put on clothes, tighten up your hair, use lip color. I don't know what that is for you. For me, I needed romance. That included date night, personal attention, vacations, and surprises. I honestly think I did a great job showing Charles romance. Guess we will have to wait to hear from him. By the Grace of God, I survived. I don't like what I went through, and I wouldn't recommend doing it the way I did it. I made it because my faith sustained me. ***He's Able. That is the next book coming soon!***

Conversationalist Delphia Sheila is a Published Author, Panelist, Speaker, Accountability Coach and Lover of God. After going through trials and tribulations and growing in the grace and knowledge of the Word, she is ready to assist women as they journey through the storms of this thing called life. With decades in the health industry helping people, along with various lessons learned, her intentional focus is mature women who find themselves struggling with their marriage, relationships, in the midst of divorce or newly divorced.

Many women devote their lives to their spouse, children, job, church, only to wake up one day and find themselves alone, seemingly without purpose. It is during those moments they can feel lost or abandoned. Delphia Sheila helps to shift that mindset from frustration and disappointment and leads them back on road to feeling whole again.

Delphia Sheila's speaking topics include Clarity, Patience, Endurance, Self-Care, and other topics along the way that we need to survive. She also offers Mentorship and serves as an Accountability Partner.

Her hobbies include Exercising, Learning Methods To Eat Fresh and Lean, Music, Movies and Growing into the Exciting World of Technology. She loves spending time with her besties and family, including her son Kalyan, two precious grandchildren, Destiny and Amaya.

Kept By His Grace

Jackie 'Lady J' Miller

The LORD is my rock, my fortress, and my deliverer, my God, my mountain where I seek refuge, my shield and the horn of my salvation, my stronghold. (Psalm 18:2 NIV)

One after one, I popped them in my mouth like they were from a pack of Skittles only these weren't sweet nor were they full of fruit flavor. I kept swallowing them because I wanted the pain to go away; I needed it to stop. I popped another one, losing count. Had it been five or six? I didn't know how many I had taken, but the point all along was to take all of them, every last sleeping pill my stomach could handle.

To say I was in a depressed state would have been an understatement. I had hit rock bottom in a loveless marriage, or rather my ex-husband refusing to love me or touch me. I still loved him though, that emotional, gut-wrenching soul tie that I clung to for dear life with all of my being, only to be tossed aside as if I didn't exist.

I heard him on the phone in the bathroom one night telling his friend how much I repulsed him, and he wouldn't touch me with a ten-foot pole. At only five-foot two inches tall, I was tipping the scale at three hundred pounds because I had gained so much weight after having his third child, but I guess I was supposed to lose it the next day.

At that time, I worked for the County health department in the Women, Infants, and Children's (WIC) program. Women were coming in for services, and I could barely concentrate on their requests. They needed help *and so did I*! My emotions were out of control. I was constantly crying, carrying around shame, frustration, confusion and disappointment in myself and what had become of my life and my marriage. All of this caused me to shut down and eventually, I struggled just to be able to get out of bed. After several unwarranted absences, I got fired and at that time, I didn't care if I lived or died. Rejection had captured me: *Why am I not enough? What is wrong with me? Am I not worthy?* These phrases coursed through my mind over and over again!

My ex literally ignored my fragile state. He flaunted his other life in my face on social media with pictures of him all hugged up with other women as if he was carefree and single. I'd stare at those posts completely embarrassed, as his infidelity chipped away at my soul. And to think I had given him my youth by marrying him at the age of seventeen.

Sometimes, life can hurt us so badly that it actually hurts to hurt!

It would seem that a Christian's life should be a life where your mind and heart are at peace. For some, this is rarely experienced. Behind closed doors, the lives of the faithful are filled with such things as anxiety, phobias, depression, worthlessness, obsessions, insecurity, rejection, guilt, bitterness, and feeling unloved. We just hold it in, trying to pray it away and handle it alone.

God didn't design the human body to deal with emotional pain day after day. Many of us are not equipped to go through so much catastrophic turmoil. I used to not understand or fathom the notion of suicide. I was at the point that ending it would prevent me from having to wake up another day to the same unfaithful dagger twisting in my heart.

I can say that issues with my ex was just one part of the puzzle. The emotional baggage from my past built a rocky foundation that I had never truly repaired.

 My story, I imagine, is not too unfamiliar, being a woman of color in a world that still struggles to see me as I am and as God created me to be. I knew early on in life that I was different, not just the anointing on my life or because my mother (the smartest woman that ever walked the earth) and my grandmother, a female Pastor, told me so. I looked different and was treated different because of it. Both of my parents were African American, yet my mother passed for Caucasian. Her soft skin was a creamy milk, and she had a small nose and thin lips. She was tall, slender, with a full chest, yet the prettiest legs I'd ever seen. My father was a dark knight, tall and statuesque-like.

Both sets of my grandparents were mixed either with Caucasian or a variation of Lumbee or Blackfoot Indian. My father's mother was a short, beautiful chocolate woman with long, shiny jet-black hair, and her mother was a beautiful blackberry woman with captivating almond-shaped eyes. My father's father was a short man with slick wavy hair, and he had a lisp when he spoke.

My mother's mother was tall, straight, and had a creamy peanut-butter-brown complexion. Her father was a dark man of average size and height. My grandfather was deceased by the time I was born, but his father, my great-grandfather was a mix of Caucasian and Lumbee Indian with light hazel eyes.

All three of my siblings were tall, with big bright eyes. My younger sister was the only one who mirrored my mother's characteristics. My brothers resembled our father to the fullest.

I'm sharing all of these details because I did not fit the mold. I was the odd one out. I spent many hours wondering, *where did I come from*? Second to the oldest, I am short, thick, and curvy with confused hair and slanted eyes that can't be seen when I smile. My own family teased me growing up, saying my parents were the owners of the Chinese food joint on the corner. They called me "thunder thighs," "China Girl," "fatty, fatty two by four, can't get through the kitchen door" and as you can imagine, my tweens and teens were the worst years for me growing up.

We have all been raised and live in a society where a lot of emphasis is put on your physical *appearance, and if you don't look a certain way, you can easily develop low self-esteem*. You see, I was *different looking*. "Black-A-Nees" they would call me, and I was thick in all the not-so-popular ways back then for my teenage group. While my other friends were dating, I didn't get my first boyfriend until I was well over fifteen years old. He was older and could appreciate my thickness and the mystery of my uniquely slanted eyes on a brown girl, or so he said. However, as a virgin, I wasn't ready for sex, so he said I didn't love him; he cheated and made a baby somewhere else then dumped me. Little did I know that a similar future awaited me because later on in life my now ex-husband would do the same. As I said, he had love for other women throughout our eighteen years of marriage. The baby boy that was the result of his infidelity activities was the child he chose to be an active father to, excluding being a husband and father to the three children born within our then marriage.

Having been raised in a deeply rooted Christian family full of Deacons, Evangelists and Pastors, I knew the Word of God and had a relationship with Him of my own at one point. But when I got older, I strayed from my faith and fell for a man for whom I was "unequally yoked" with, as my Pastor Grandmother would tell me. With her gifts of prophesy and insight, she would constantly tell me to leave him alone because he didn't believe in the God we served. I didn't listen; I had to learn the hard way. So there I was, taking a bunch of sleeping pills, hearing her in hindsight saying, "eventually, eeee...ventually" meaning I would find out.

After not succeeding in my first attempt at suicide, because within an hour I was vomiting profusely all over myself, I found out the hard way that Haldol, Tylenol PM, a whole pepperoni pizza and alcohol was a bad combination. I called for my neighbor, Janet, who was the closest in proximity to me. In turn, she called my husband,

and he could have cared less. It was then that I realized ....''Eventually" had finally come!

Later, due to my unstable state, I had a second nervous breakdown, and that put me in the psychiatric unit for 30 days. Being separated from my three heart beats was sheer torture. Up until that point, they were the only thing keeping me sane. Truth be told they kept me from focusing on how horrible and disgusting I felt all because of the man I was so madly in love with was a habitual cheater, manipulative and conniving. He had me convinced it was my fault he had so many other women. He berated me by telling me how fat and ugly I was. How I let myself continue to take him back and then give him a child three times over I can't explain, but the cliché is true: love is blind. Please understand my children are truly the best part of me, so I don't regret it at all.

During the thirty days of me trying to reclaim my sanity, it led to us having a ten-month separation, and I ended up being a single mother in every sense of the phrase. I even loss eighty pounds, but I was still walking around with blinders on, unable to see that he had me in the worst kind of chokehold, where I believed that no one else could possibly want me...ever. So, I attended alone (because he was an atheist) six weeks of marriage counseling with my pastor to re-commit to this man in a vow renewal ceremony. I was under the false pretense that I could save him and make him love me, that we could become the fairy tale all little girls dream about of being a happy family and growing old together.

We remarried in September 1999 with an elaborate wedding. Two months later in November, he had beaten me and put me and the children out in the street. In an instant, we were homeless, but thankfully family took us in until I was able to be self-sufficient.

While that was devastating and humiliating, I must admit that I was stronger in that season of my life because I had already had multiple nervous breakdowns and had years of weekly counseling with an amazing psychiatrist, Dr. Asher, who has since passed away. She was instrumental in finding the real me.

Even though I was on the road to healing from my emotional pain, there was still a void that had to be filled. I had come to the realization that God has the ultimate cure for my emotional pain. The Lord called me back into the fold and my journey led me back to church. I convinced myself that he had changed and to give him another chance; after all, God forgives us over and over again, and He casts our transgressions into the sea of forgetfulness, right? Seriously, he would bring me flowers, tell me how much he loved me, spend time with the children and I, and bring us on trips. I hadn't fully learned at that point that the word of God didn't make a difference to him because he didn't believe in God to begin with, but I thought my faith, prayers and love was enough for the both of us.

After that big wedding in front of almost two hundred guests, and then to be homeless two months later, I couldn't bring myself to go back to the church I loved for nearly three years. Not because of anything someone else did or said, but simply because of the voices in my head, which were filled with negativity: *People are going to be talking about you; with no husband, they won't accept you; you didn't try hard enough.* As much as I thought I was okay with the divorce, I still felt like a failure, embarrassed and ashamed.

In those years, the struggle was real. I spent years trying to make it on my own, giving myself completely over to God. It was truly the only course of action that I had.

Unfortunately, many who go through the trauma of emotional pain are not always quick or willing to seek help or do anything about it, whether it is secular or spiritual. You know in some Black communities, it is taboo to admit that you need professional help. Instead, we will choose to continue to wallow in our pain. As one who has experienced depression, I know how difficult it is to open up to others about emotional pain.

We are quick to feel like someone will think we are mentally unbalanced. Of course, this may not be true, but we will use it as our reasoning and justification as to why we can't and won't get help. The emotional pain I mentioned above had no connection with me being "crazy" yet I did feel like that's what others would think of me.

Like me, some feel they can work through it or "snap out of it." Others are afraid they will reveal damaging family secrets. No doubt some refuse professional help because of the expense involved; finances shouldn't dictate your ability to obtain help for emotional wellness.

A healthy emotional state is one of the foundations of overall wellbeing. It may take a long time, but it is yours for the taking. In fact, I can guarantee you that if you will submit to the guidance of a licensed professional, along with the cure provided directly by God, you can soon divest yourself of painful emotions.

It is imperative that we turn that critical inner voice that we all listen to into an ongoing opportunity for self-love, positivity, and growth. We have to stop letting the "enemy" use the "inner-me" to sabotage us. The expression "you are your own worst enemy" is fairly true for most of us at some point in our lives. Self-reflect: Do you self-sabotage relationships, your finances, your career or all of the above? We have to ask ourselves the hard questions and be truthful in response. You see self-sabotaging thoughts and behaviors manifest into our reality, i.e., if I keep telling myself I'm fat and unattractive then I won't see myself any other way. This kind of "stinking thinking" will shut down every opportunity for you to succeed at anything. One of my mindset coaches, Deborah, told us that "all self-sabotage, lack of belief in oneself, low self-esteem, judgments, criticism and the demands for perfection are forms of self-abuse which destroy the very essence of our vitality." Once you see you have room for improvement, then allow yourself the grace to work at it each day. So STOP the self-sabotage cycle.

For starters, we have to understand that emotional health is not the same thing as mental health. Yes, the two terms are often used interchangeably. Emotional health "focuses on being in tune with our emotions, vulnerability, and authenticity," says licensed psychologist Juli Fraga, PsyD[1]. Having good emotional health truly is a fundamental aspect of building resilience, self-awareness, and overall contentment. Keep in mind that having good emotional health doesn't mean you're always happy or free from negative emotions. It's about having the ability, skills and resources to manage the ups and downs of our day-to-day life.

How do we go from the feelings of total despair and defeat to survivor? For me, I went BACK to my rock, wholeheartedly! The true source of my strength. Because even in my brokenness, He was still there providing, protecting and guiding me. God's word was and still "is a lamp for my feet and a light on my path." (Psalm 119:105 NIV) The B.I.B.L.E. is **B**asic **I**nstructions **B**efore **L**eaving **E**arth. It is full of reminders and encouragement for living and surviving life.

In one of His sermons Jesus said, "I have come that they may have life, and that they may have it more abundantly" (John 10:10 NIV) It is clear that Jesus is saying he can offer us a more abundant way of living than what we have been experiencing. God's intention is that Christians have a good life that is free, overflowing, adventurous and exciting beyond any other kind of existence. He wants to provide us with love, peace, joy and security.

When you start to feed yourself the true Bread of Life, what you receive back out is what God has designed, which is to live peacefully, loving life, and full of joy. You will come to recognize that negative thoughts and behavior are sometimes the results of choices that we have made. You will learn to choose differently from what you have been doing. You will begin to daily renew your mind, your thoughts will change, and in doing so, even your language and actions will change. A quote I like from Author Neil T Anderson, "The more you reaffirm who you are in Christ, the more your behavior will begin to reflect your true identity.²"

You have to speak life over yourself. Daily affirmations, such as "I can do all things through Christ who strengthens me," "I am a conqueror," "I am wonderful and fearfully made," will help you Survive anything. With all I have been through, if I'm able to wake each day with praise on my lips and joy in my heart, you can too.

#Yougothis   #Speaklife   #HisGraceissufficent #YouareASurvivor #KeptByHisGrace

- ¹www.healthinfi.com licensed psychologist Juli Fraga, PsyD.
- ²Neil T. Anderson, Dave Park (2008). "Stomping Out the Darkness: Discover Your True Identity in Christ and Stop Putting Up with the World's Garbage!"

 **Jacqueline B. Miller "Lady J"** is a creative, energetic multi-faceted Woman of God. Answering "the call" she feels is by far the greatest accomplishment of her life. As an ordained Minister of the Gospel, a Couples Coach, Life Coach, Writer, Published Author and virtual talk show personality, you will find that she has a servant's heart. Loving and caring for God's people is the fundamental foundation she stands on.

Lady J is the creator and founder of the Internet talk show, Victory Talk. She finds so much joy in helping others learn to #Speaklife and share their accomplishments as they grow to their next level. She does her best to fulfill her desire to motivate and inspire others to live a victorious life. **Lady J's** initiative and determination keeps her focused. Her resilience is her primary motivation to glorify God and her edification of others.

She and husband, Pastor Phillip A. Miller, Sr. of Victorious Living Faith (VLF): Not Your

Traditional Church, work diligently to bring about change in the lives of God's people and communities. **Lady J** has a passion for marriages and helping couples to grow while keeping the fires hot! Along with her husband, they have been leading the "Yes Marriage Works; If You Work It" ministry for over 14 years.

As Co-Pastor of VLF, she prefers staying in the background where she can encourage and serve God's people with complete anonymity. Overall **Lady J** is very comfortable leading from the second chair.

Jacqueline's most humble service to God has been as a wife, a mother of six children and grandmother of three grandchildren. She believes living the example before them is her most challenging yet rewarding mission in life.

CONTACT: Jacqueline B. ~Jackie "Lady J" Miller:

On the web: http://Vlfminstrys.org/

Facebook: @ victorytalk
or https://www.facebook.com/jackie.y.miller

Twitter: @JackieLadyJ1.

Instagram: JackieLadyJ1/   Jackie Miller
Email: jmblessedevents@vlfministrys.org

Lady J 🌹

...."Don't allow your past to rob you of your future"
...I can do all thigs through Christ who strengthens me...

Philippians 4:13
...If you have Faith, nothing shall be impossible for you...Matthew 17:20

Reclaiming Your Destiny

J C Gardner

So many of us are planted in the wrong garden. We started out being a rose and then ended up as a pine tree and more often than not, it was because you ended up being planted where someone else thought you should be vs. where you were *destined* to be.

Make no mistake, we all have a divine purpose, as we have been infused with various gifts and talents by the Creator. Some of us are late bloomers, so these characteristics will surface later in life where others know early on just exactly why type of flower they were meant to be. Yet, they ended up in the wrong field (pun intended!)

I'm speaking from experience. At the age of twelve, I knew I was to be an author, a crafter of words, an entertainer through the power of the pen. I recall that revelation day like it was yesterday where me and my BFF spent a week's vacation with my grandmother. After about five days, though, we were bored, and I suggested we write stories. She agreed but after twenty minutes, my pages were filled and hers were blank.

Right then and there, I knew in my heart and mind I was to be an author.

Words came to me easily. Being an only child for ten years, I had a ton of imaginary friends who told me all of their secrets and once I started writing, I couldn't stop! It was like the floodgates of knowledge opened, and I poured it all onto the pages, dubbing each story, song, or play "my masterpiece."

So while the seeds of discovery were germinating and still taking root, I entered seventh grade. If you see me now, you probably think I was always loud, funny, direct and confident. That is because later in life I had a God-formation, aka transformation, but back then...I was shy, nervous, quiet, and somewhat introverted. I knew God, but at that young age, my spiritual walk was still a work in progress. When my English teacher assigned a creative writing project, I was ecstatic and could not wait to share with her my original book of poems.

See, I already knew that my writing would speak for me. It would tell people who I was. My expressive words would introduce me to whoever would lend an ear to hear. It was to be my ticket to self-confidence, awareness, and would allow me to have a voice.

I handed in my book of poetry and waited for her critique. I had visions of getting an A. I would have accepted a B+, but I was aiming for *thee* A and more importantly, the English teacher, who barely paid any attention to me, would finally know my name.

On that fateful day when the assignments were returned, mine was returned last – well it was thrown on my desk. If you've heard me speak on this subject, you know what happened next. She announced to the class I would be given a zero, that there was no way I wrote those poems. As if that wasn't enough damage, she went on to say they were plagiarized!

If you are a writer of any kind, just mentioning the word **plagiarized** is like a dagger to the heart. Plagiarize means stolen, copied, bootlegged, lifted. Basically, I didn't write them.

To say I was crushed and humiliated would be an understatement. Just as my destiny -- my divine assignment -- was about to bloom, all of the leaves wilted, and the petals flew into the wind. Her hateful and hurtful words replaced my creative seeds with thorny weeds and those weeds grew and choked the life out of me to the point where I became a closet writer for decades. Yes, decades. I was a prisoner of someone else's mind.

Let's pause here for a moment and let me throw a curve ball your way.

I hope you are able to see *the beauty* in all of this. It took me awhile to even acknowledge there was beauty in my pain and here is the awesomeness of God: **I never stopped writing**.

The reason why I became a closet writer is because writing for me was like an extra but necessary body part. Once I had opened up my God-given gift and it took root, only HE could shut it down. So the words continued to pour out of me like summer rains on a hot day. Every now and then, I would share a farewell poem for a colleague or some other small, anecdotal writings, but I wouldn't share it any further.

I was afraid. I feared rejection. Those painful memories would rise up again and again and kept me in mental bondage. My soul could not handle another person saying I couldn't write, I wasn't worthy, I had no creativity, I'm a thief.

Even though I was petrified of rejection, the purposeful seeds would try to break through the weeds and rise up and tug at my spirit and scream at me to share my gift. I would refuse that notion, asking myself, "What's the use?"

What happened is that I had become comfortable in my grief. It's easy to stay in our mess because it's familiar and then we convince ourselves *yeah, this is where I'm supposed to be – this is where I deserve to be!* I know I'm stepping on some toes with this one but hang with me. While I sat back and watched all of the other flowers flourish in the sunlight, I was cowering down, in the darkness, comfortable in the dirt. To break free would require work, watering, nurturing and the fortitude to accept rejection and disappointment because that is part of life.

And then one day, my life changed forever. After three decades of feeling sorry for myself, God paid me a visit. Actually, I invited Him to do so. I had gone on a raucous rant of why I was not a published author. How come He had not allowed me to walk in my gift? I won't bore you with all of the details, but let's just say there was a lot of ugly crying, guilt, blame-game comments and falling out. Yes, all of that. I wanted to know why God had not blessed me and helped me where my writing was concerned, while I watched the literary careers of others take off. When that storm was over, God clearly spoke to me and asked the most profound question:

"Who have you been listening to?"

Well now, that struck a chord. What was downloaded in an instant was how for many years, I was operating under that teacher's words. **Not God's words**. I allowed myself to be tricked by the enemy into thinking that my innate gifts and talents were a waste. It had not occurred to me up until that moment that perhaps that teacher could have never written a poem to save her life so how was a twelve-year-old able to do it in her eyes? Jealousy and envy do not only surface with your peers but can also happen with authority figures, family, colleagues and even church members. She lashed out at me because of her own inadequacies. I was too young to see it then, but on the day of God's visit, it was crystal clear.

The enemy **IS NOT** about you living for God or using your gifts and talents as God intended. He is here to sow discord, confusion, strife and to keep you off your God-given assignment.

When God hit me with that knowledge, life changed forever. The weeds in my soul were replaced with fertile soil and fresh seeds. I allowed His Spirit to rain down on me until I was able to breakthrough to the other side and bloom where He intended me to be planted. Today, I'm a best-selling author, an award-winning author, writing coach, ghostwriter and inspirational speaker.

I say to you, are you in the right garden? Did you start out knowing your purpose only to be told otherwise so you took a man-made detour? Or perhaps you have found yourself living for other people, forsaking your own destiny, thinking it's too late.

As long as you have breath in your body, it's never too late.

This is not my saying but I believe it to be true. Just how many gifts, talents, and ideas are in the cemetery? Don't take yours to the grave. Someone is waiting on you to show up. Someone needs you in their life because what He gave you is there for a reason. Every day you hold on to it is another lost blessing to yourself and others.

I want to help you get to the right garden. It will take work and maybe some tears and a few setbacks, but in the end, it will be worth it and you will be more fulfilled on your life journey. Here are three steps to reclaim your destiny on the road to living your authentic life:

1. **Pray, meditate and reflect on what it is you are supposed to be doing**. If every day you wake up and know that the day ahead is not fulfilling or you have to force yourself to just get moving, that is a clear indication you need to be repotted. You need a fresh start. Get clarity on your purpose because then you will be able to implement baby steps to achieving that goal.

2. **Make a contract with yourself on the new revelation**. Whatever clarity you received during your prayer or meditative time, write it down. For example, "Today, I am clear that my life's purpose is to open a bakery." Now that you've gotten confirmation on your "why," you can now start to act on it. One action step is to write down all of the things you would need to start that business. Another is to actually speak to someone who is already doing what you aspire to do and learn from them.
3. **Join or create a support group**. You are not supposed to be on this journey alone. If you have not been operating in your gift(s) for a long time, this mindset shift will be a bit easier with help from those in your circle who can be there to uplift, guide, and give unbiased love and support.

There are many other tips and tools but doing any one of these should help jumpstart rediscovering and pursuing your purpose. **The main point is to start and keep going**.

I'm rooting for you and cheering for your breakthrough. Do not ever doubt your brilliance and what you bring to the table. You are unique, crafted, shaped and molded by the Master's hands. May you now feel empowered to go forth and walk boldly in your gifts.

Spiritual Reflections (NIV):

Ephesians 2:10: For we are God's handiwork, created in Christ Jesus to do good works, which God prepared in advance for us to do.

1 Peter 4:10: Each of you should use whatever gift you have received to serve others, as faithful stewards of God's grace in its various forms.

Romans 12:6-8: We have different gifts, according to the grace given to each of us. If your gift is prophesying, then prophesy in accordance with your faith; if it is serving, then serve; if it is teaching, then teach; if it is to encourage, then give encouragement; if it is giving, then give generously; if it is to lead, do it diligently; if it is to show mercy, do it cheerfully.

Psalm 139:14: I praise you because I am fearfully and wonderfully made; your works are wonderful, I know that full well.

 **JC Gardner** is an author, an international speaker, writing coach and ghost writer. Helping aspiring authors bring their projects to life through her coaching program is a blessing and a gift. She has written and co-authored numerous books, along with contributing to many publications. Her latest novel, "Heated," is an urban dramedy about a single mother's plight to do better despite her negative circumstances. It is the recipient of an IPPY Award, a Distinguished Author's Guild Award, and an Amazon best seller.

JC was a closet writer for many years due to a devastating blow in her past that silenced her creativity and almost derailed her God-given talent of being an entertainer and storyteller through the written word. After a phenomenal, spiritual breakthrough, it was clear that what God has placed in your heart, no one can take away. She is a natural born writer; it is infused in her D.N.A. and believes everyone's D.N.A. makes them **D**eliberately **N**ot **A**verage! After years of living in a cloud of self-doubt and fear of rejection, she uses her platform as a speaker to transform and empower women to reclaim their destiny using real life examples, practical solutions, faith and humor.

JC is a National Advisor at an international nonprofit. She has been married for over 34 years and has two successful grown children.

Stay in touch with JC:

- https://www.facebook.com/AuthorJCG

- https://www.instagram.com/author_jcg/

- www.jc-gardner.com

- authorjcg@yahoo.com

www.ingramcontent.com/pod-product-compliance
Lightning Source LLC
Chambersburg PA
CBHW022204090526
44583CB00012BA/502